Easy Mazes for Toddlers

Toddler Maze Activity Book

John B. Tutor
"Mr. Math"

This book is for your personal enjoyment only. No part of this publication may be replicated, redistributed, or given away in any form without the prior written consent of the author.

Copyright © 2019 All rights reserved worldwide.

ISBN: 9781096134107

This maze master book belongs to

_____

Help your little maze master enhance motor skills, develop problem-solving abilities and build self-confidence.

Every time a child completes a maze successfully he or she is awarded a gold star. When the mazes are completed, count the colored stars and fill in the number on the achievement certificate at the end of the book.

Practice basic pencil skills to get started.

Follow the path from start to finish.

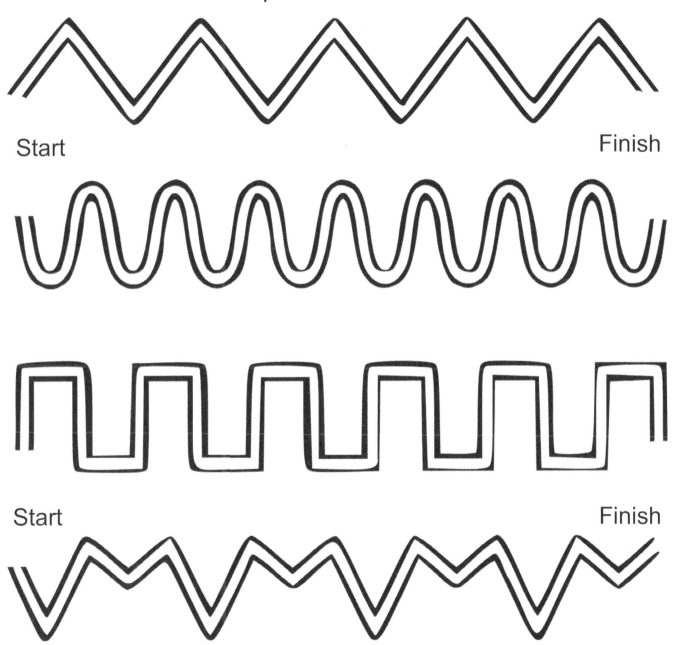

How did you do?

It was easy.

I need more practice.

I'm ready to start the mazes.

Follow the ▢ from the dog to the bone.

Draw a puppy dog then color.

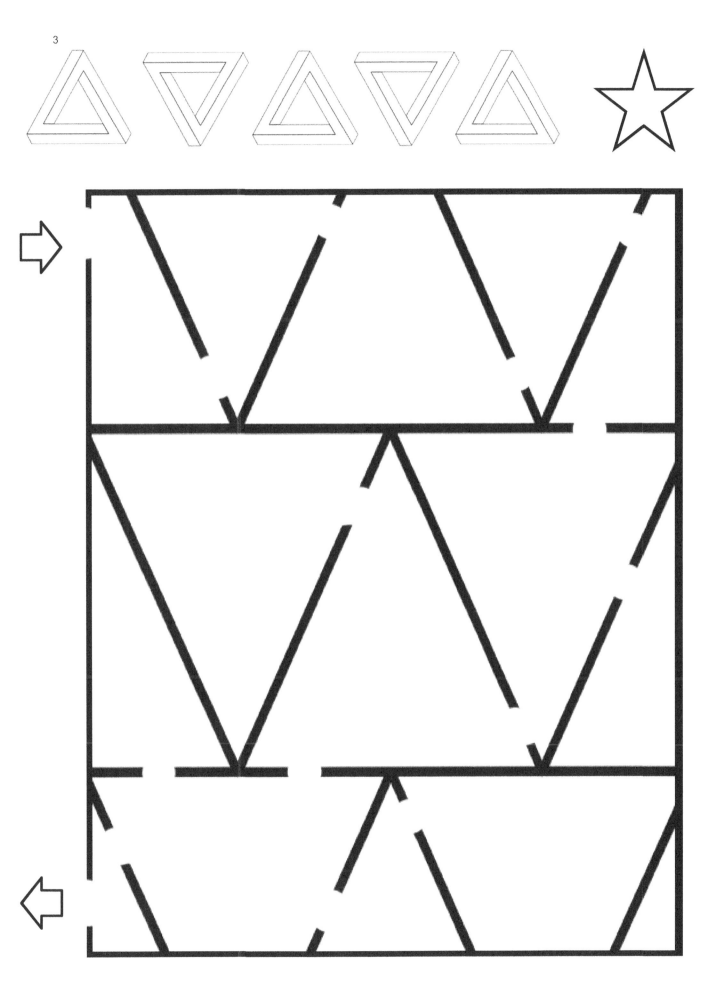

Draw a triangle.

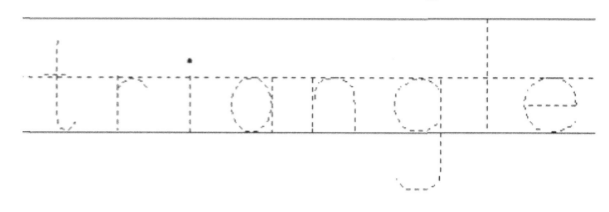

What do bunny rabbits eat?

Grass and hay

Chips and dip

Cake and ice cream

Draw a circle.

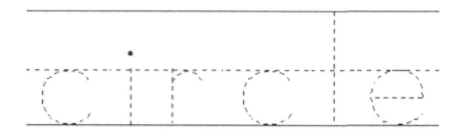

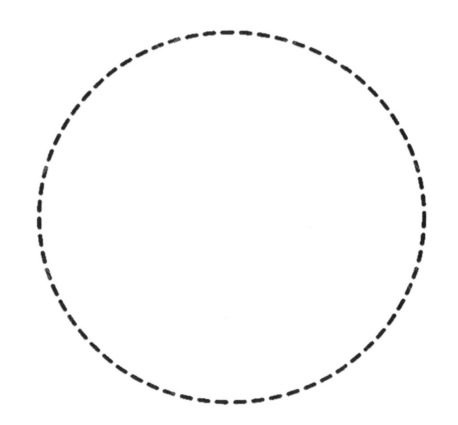

9

Draw a line to match the pictures.

What is a panda's favorite food?

Sugar cane

Eucalyptus leaves

Bamboo

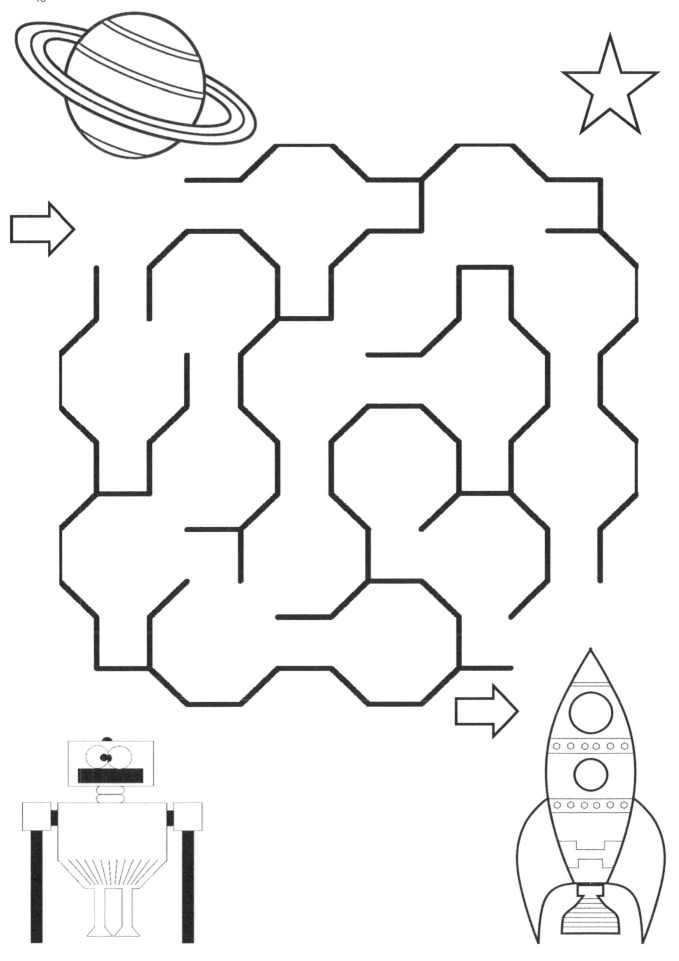

Count the robots.

Circle the correct number.

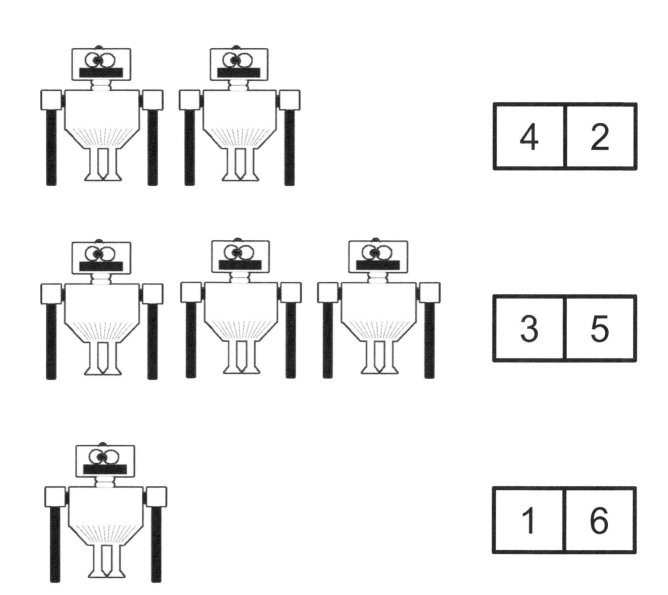

Spot the 4 differences.

Pick out the baseball.

Trace the letters by following the dots.

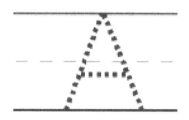

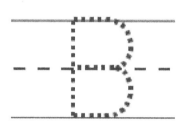

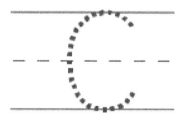

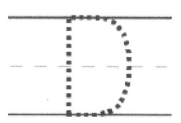

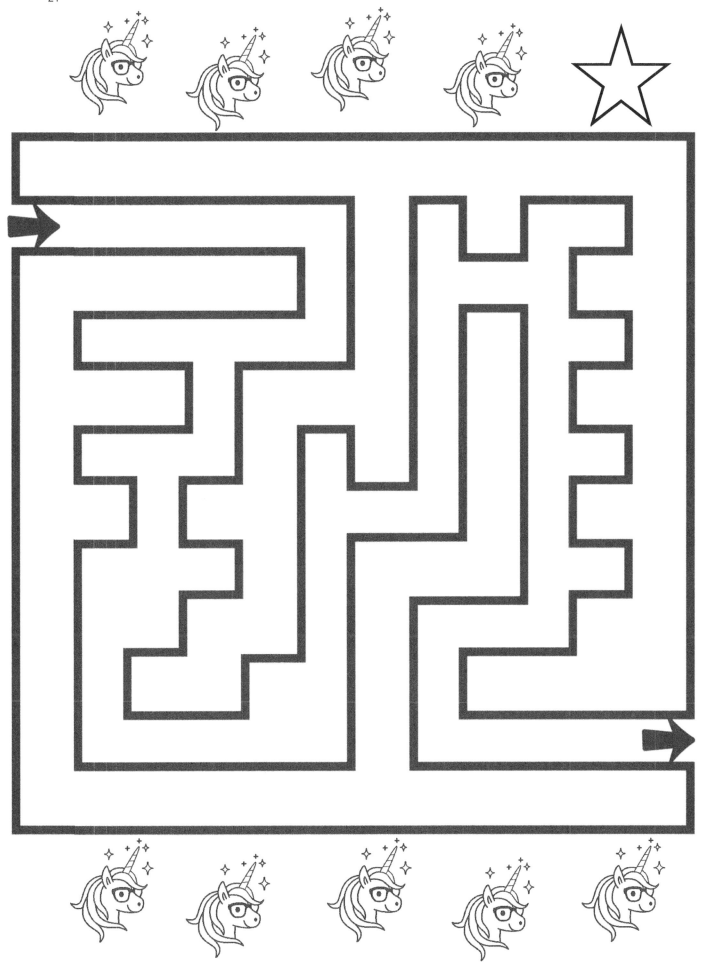

Which unicorn do you like?

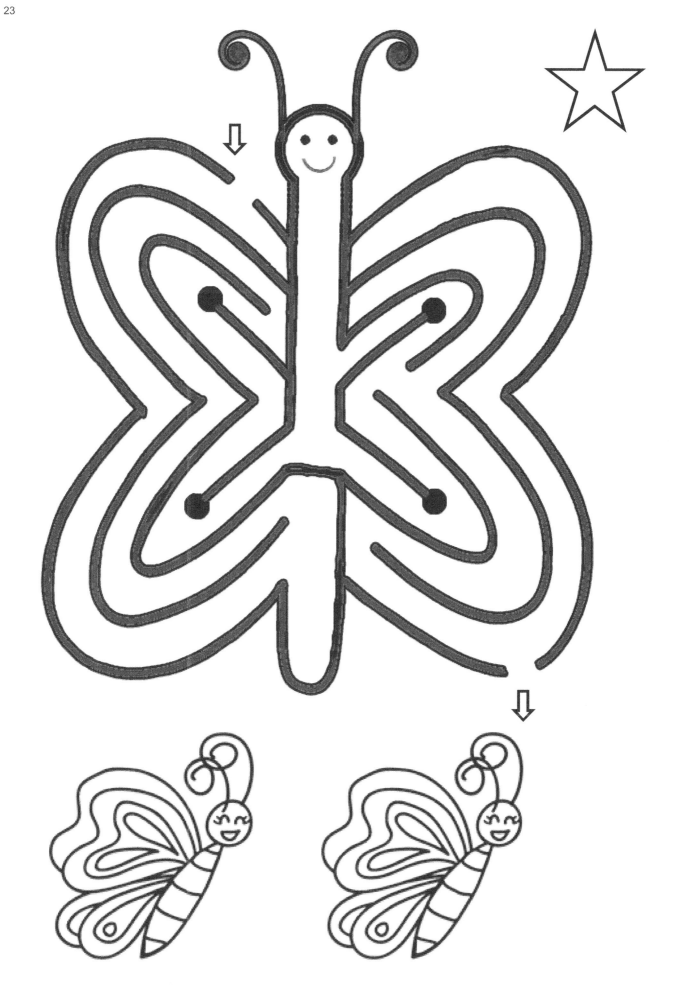

Draw a line to match the pictures.

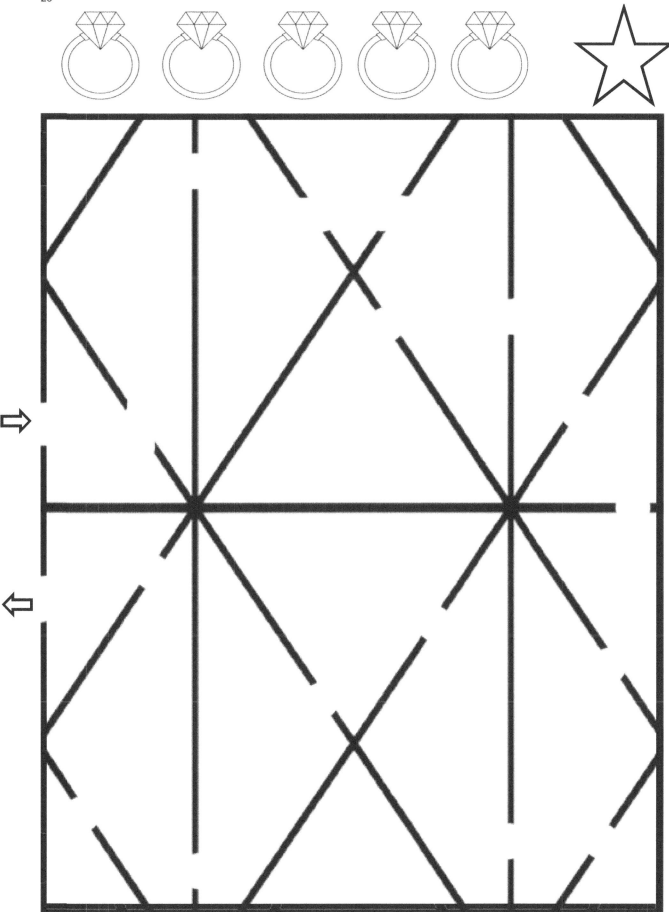

Draw a diamond.

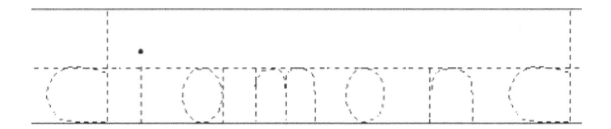

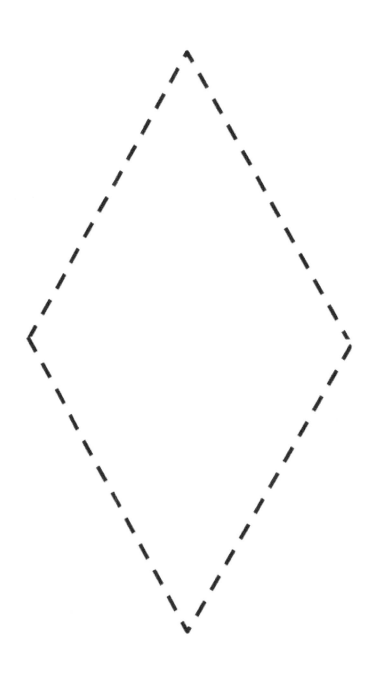

Draw a smiley face then color.

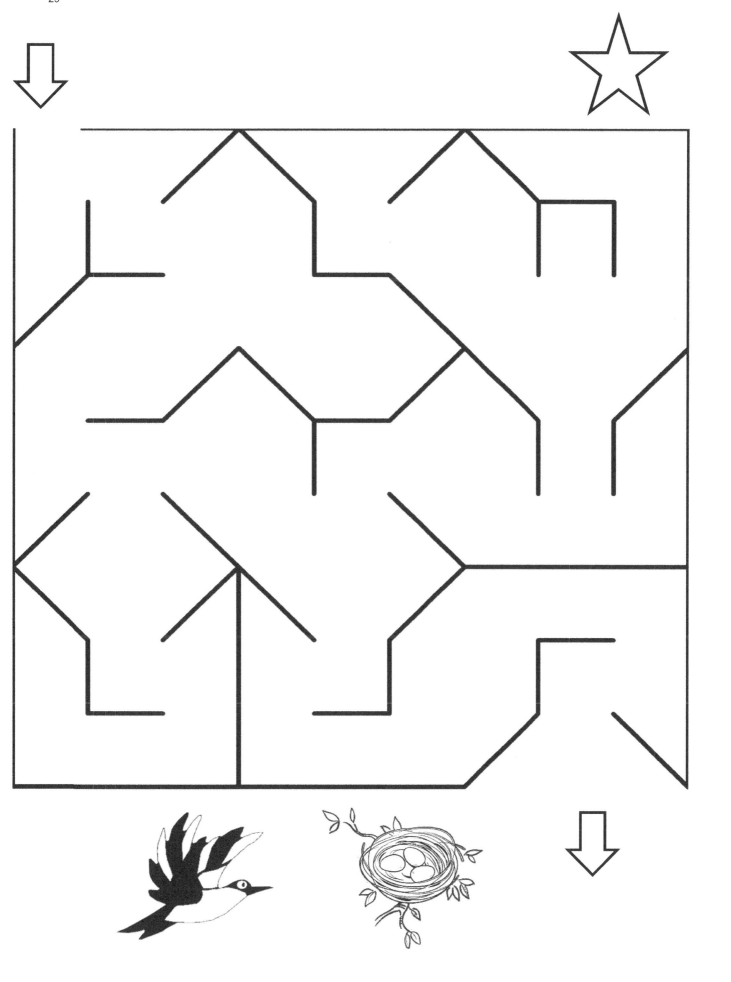

How many babies are in the nest?

3

2

1

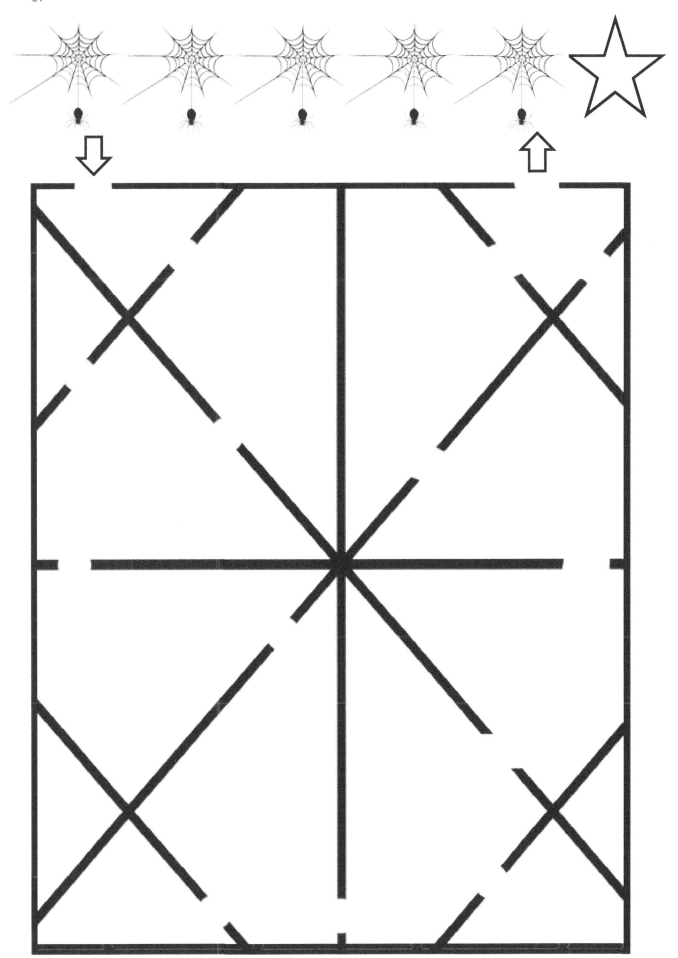

Circle the fireflies that are the same.

Can you make a zigzag pattern like this?

How many sides does a ⬡ have?

5

6

7

Which pie do you like?

Peach

Cherry

Pecan

Which picture does not belong?

41

Draw a line to match the flowers.

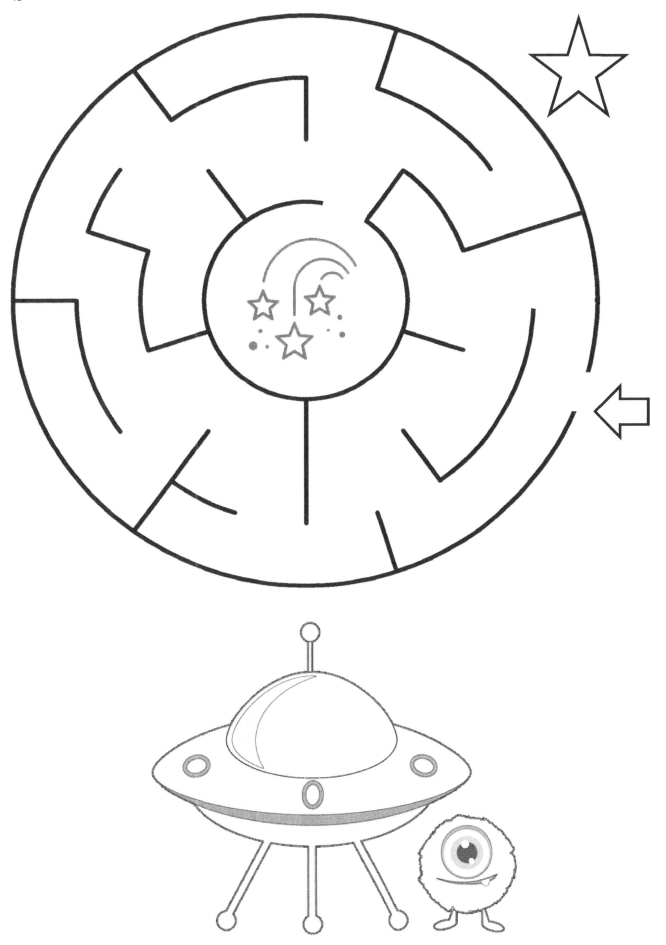

Have you ever seen a shooting star?

Yes

No

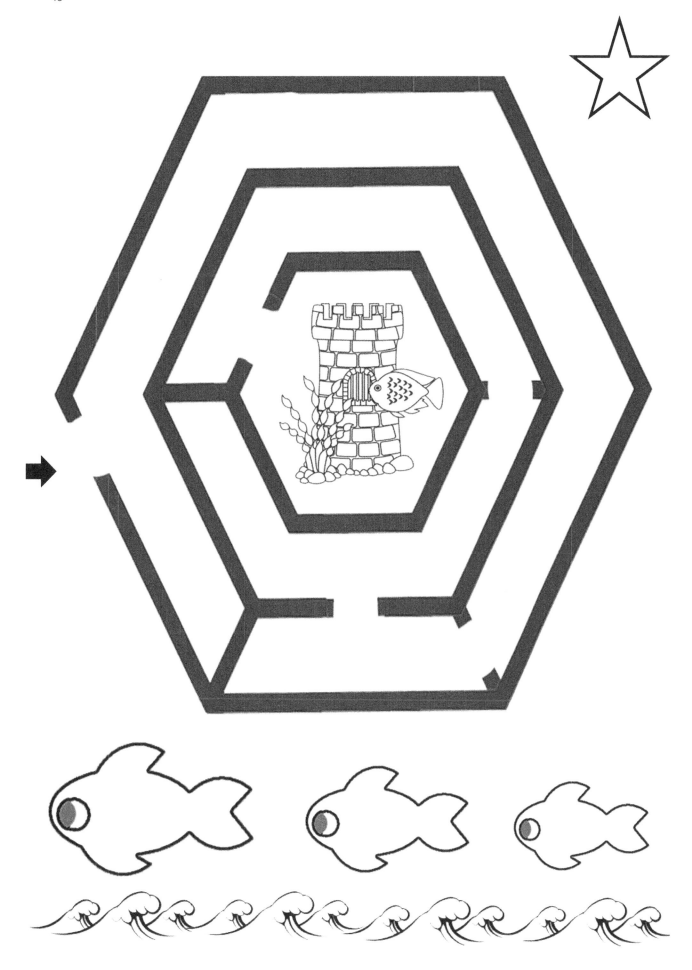

Which picture is different?

Cross out the ⊖ that are different.

Who wear ♛ crowns?

        Presidents

        Kings

        Queens

Can you draw a flower pot?

What do trains travel on?

Railroad tracks

Freeways

Dirt roads

Draw a line to match the words to the pictures.

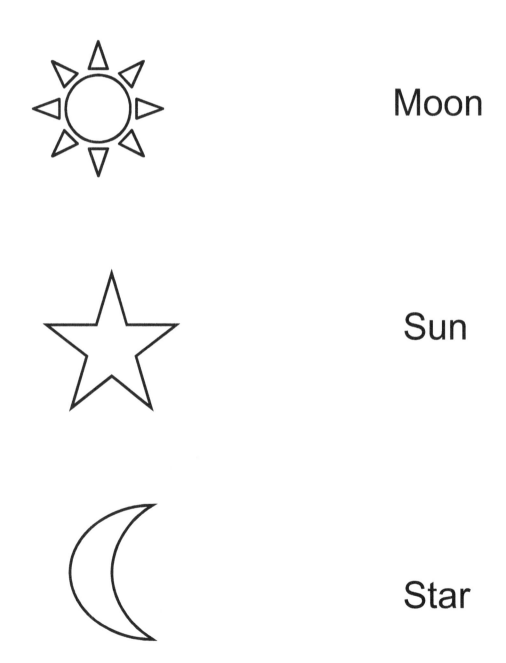

Follow the from the kids to the cards.

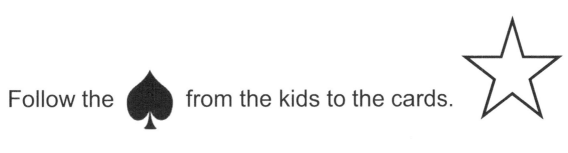

Which one is not a card game?

Old Maid and Go Fish

Jacks and Marbles

Crazy Eights And War

Play a game of Tic-tac-toe.

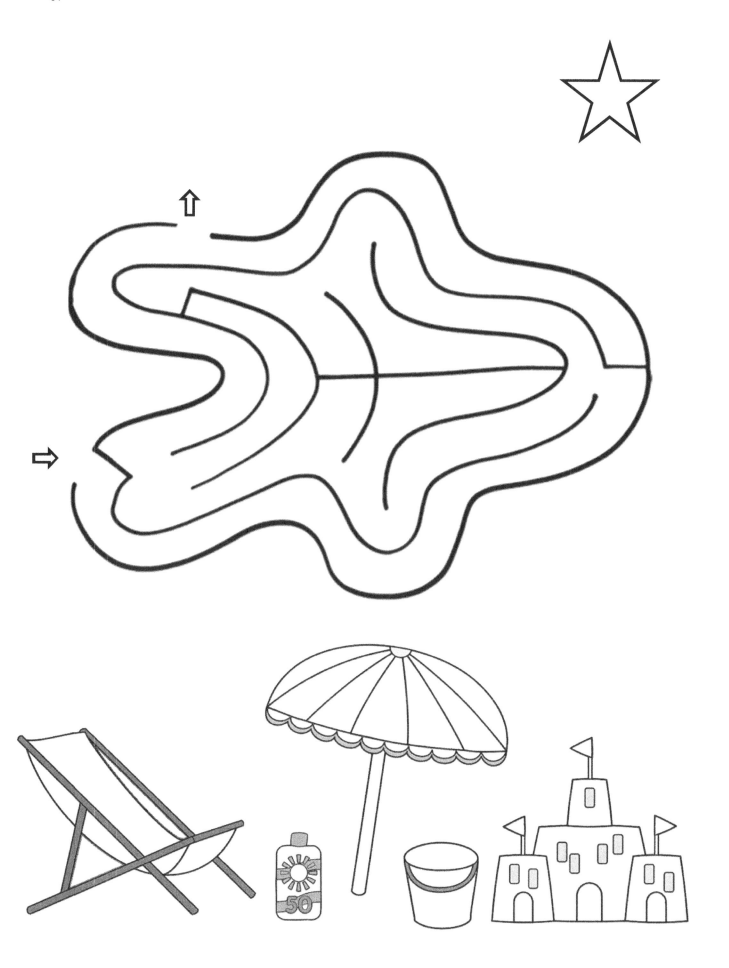

Can you draw a seahorse?

Trace the letters by following the dots.

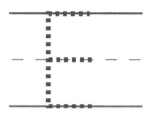

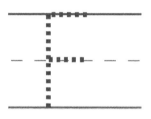

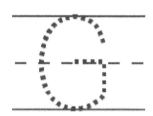

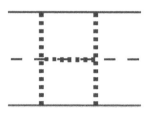

65

Trace the numbers by following the dotted lines.

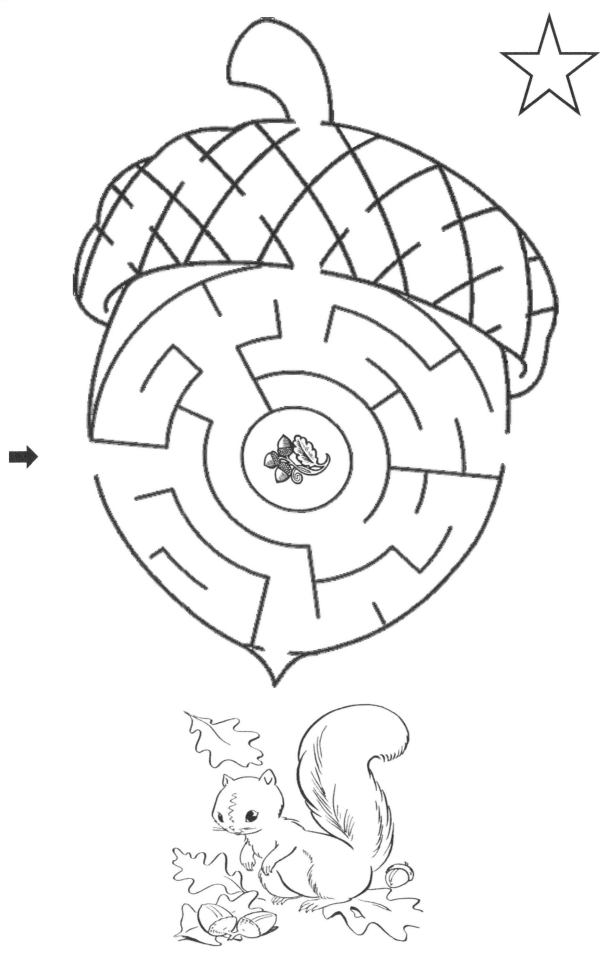

Which row does not belong?

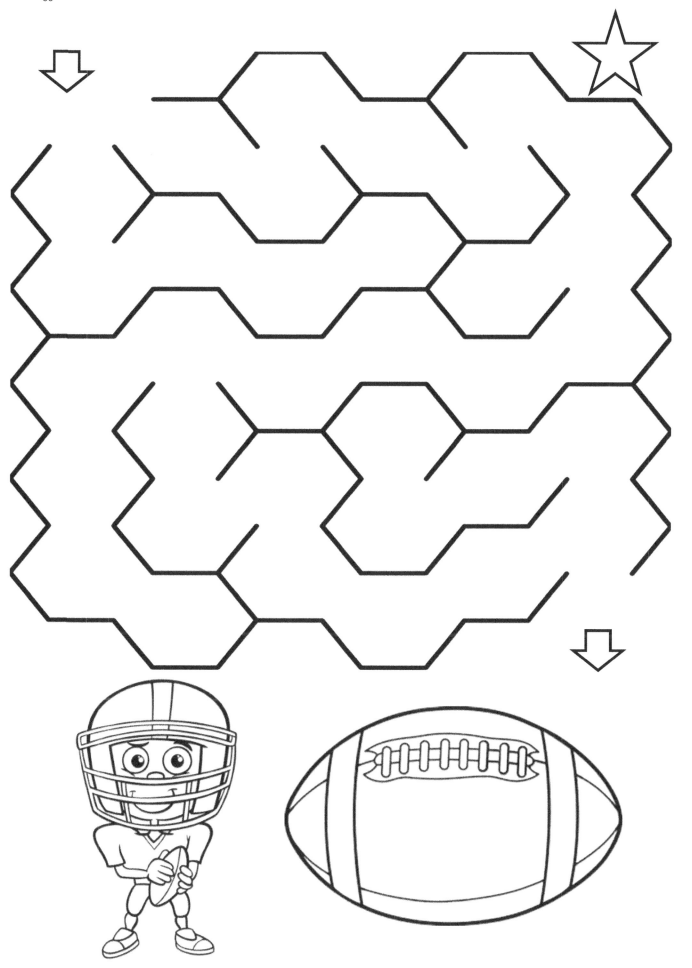

Circle the same pictures in each row.

Trace the letters by following the dots.

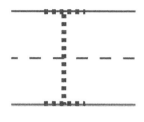

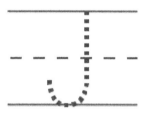

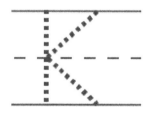

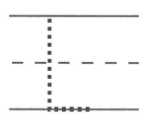

Rabbits hatch from eggs just like chickens.

True

False

Spot the 4 differences.

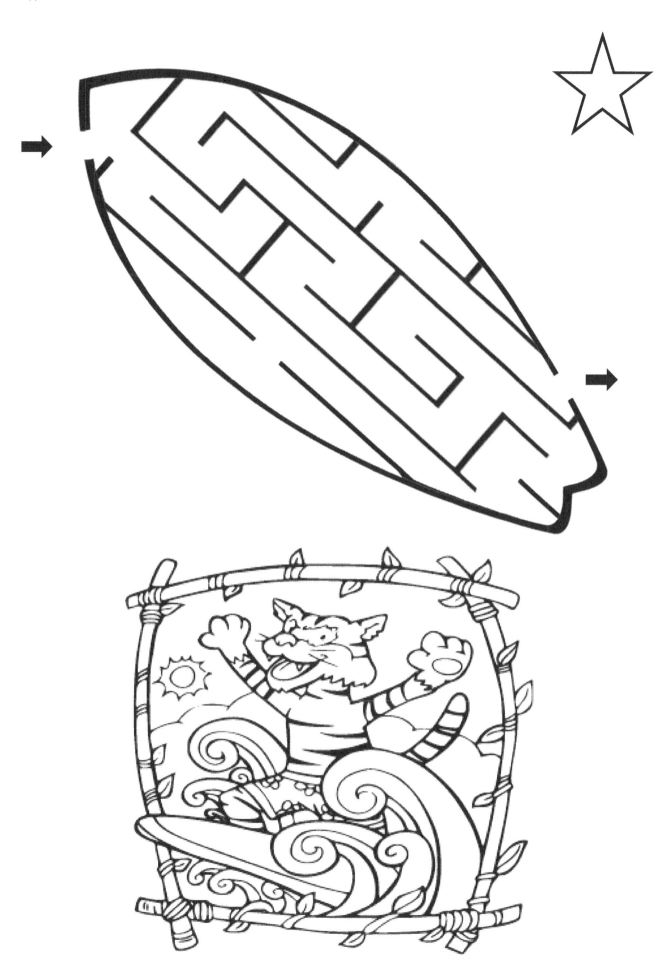

Color the cool surfing cat.

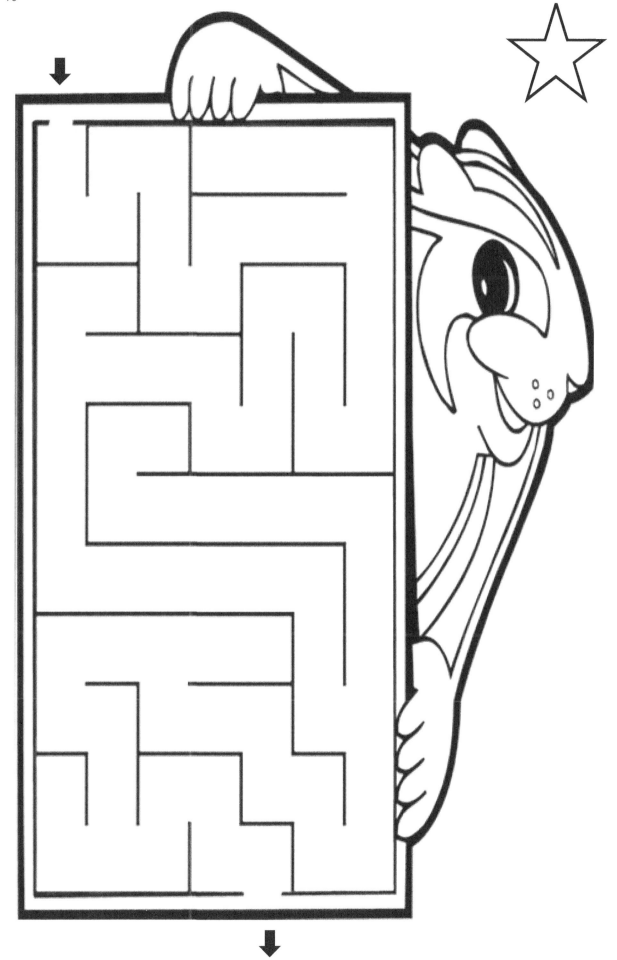

Trace the letters by following the dots.

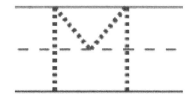

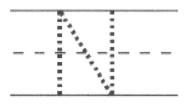

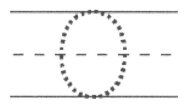

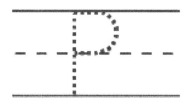

Do you like apple pie?

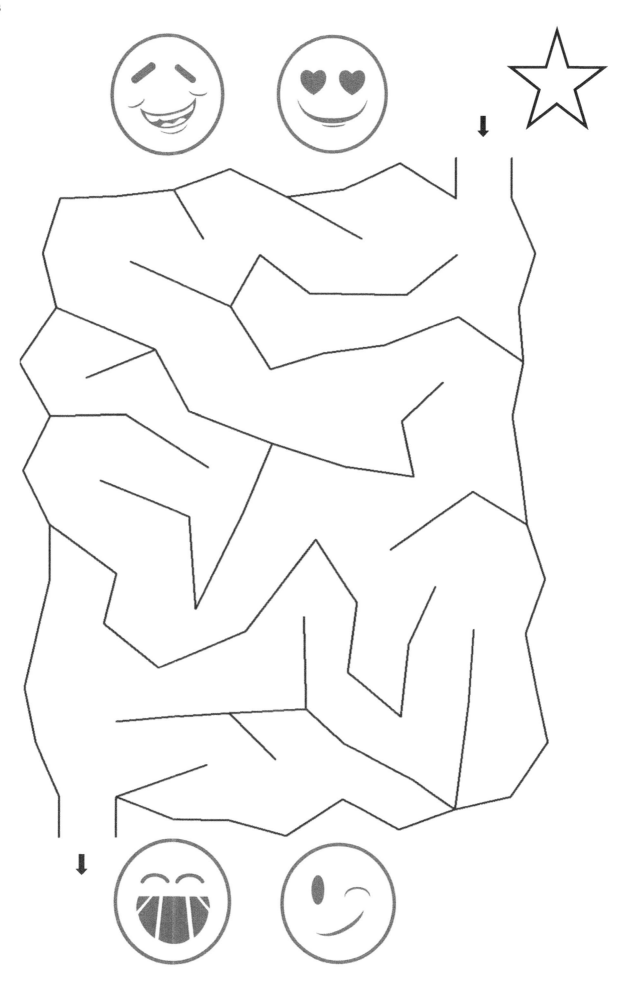

What are the square faces saying?

I'm sad.

I'm surprised.

I'm happy.

Draw a line to match the pictures.

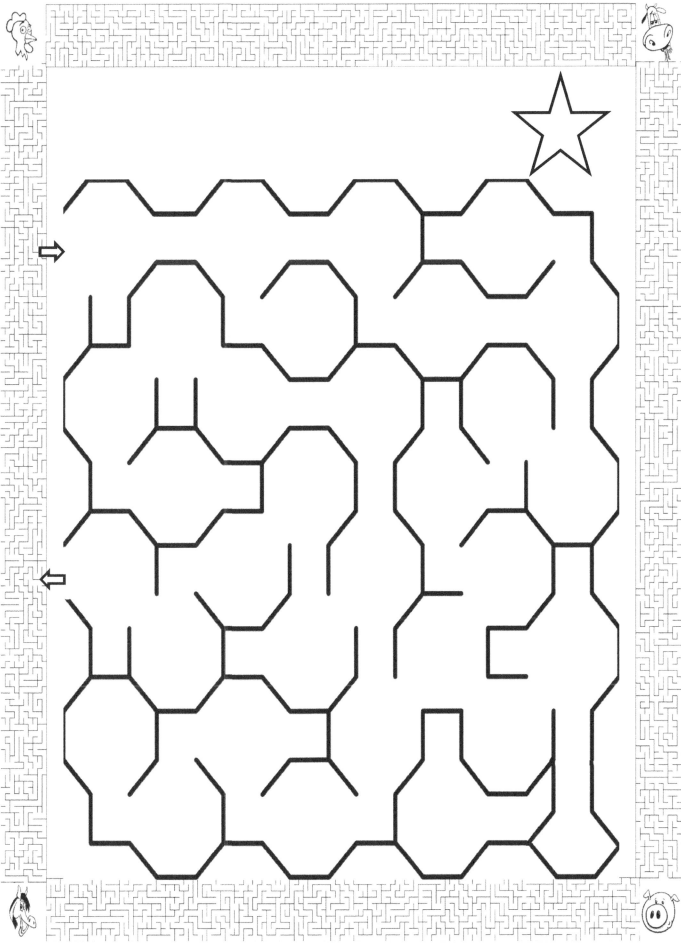

Where do eggs ⬭ come from?

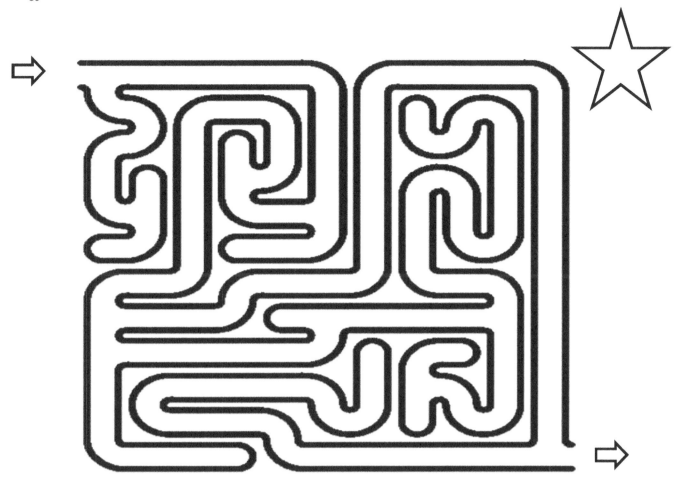

Circle the same pictures in each row.

What are the square faces saying?

I'm tired.

I'm angry.

I'm scared.

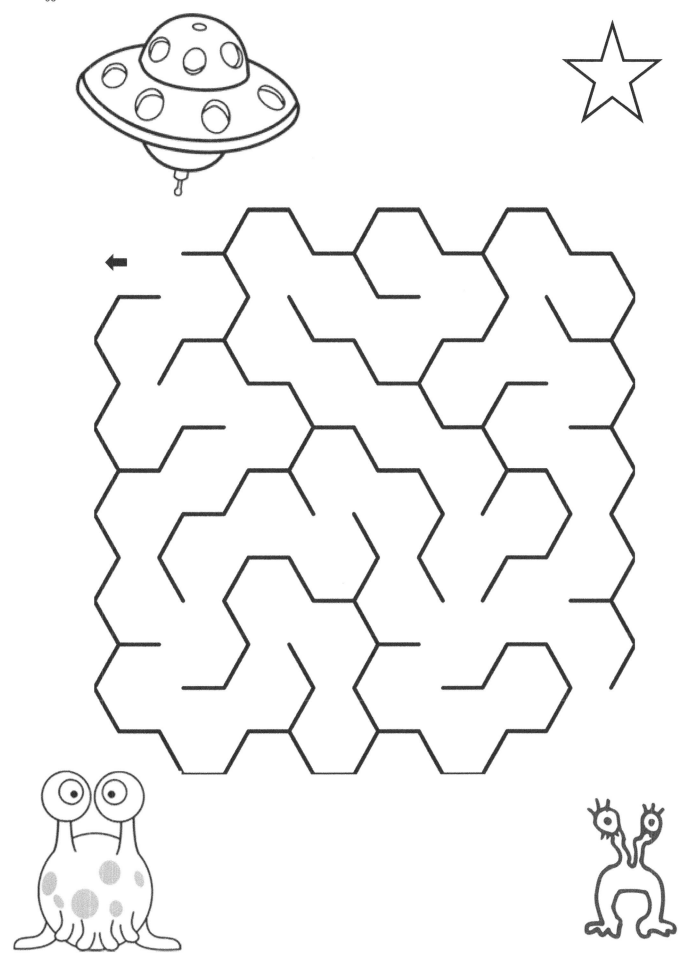

What are the aliens trying to do on the previous page?

Phone home.

Land on Earth.

Find their spaceship.

Connects the dots.

Which animal starts with the letter h?

Fill in the blank with the missing letter.

_rab

_hale

_ish

F C W

Where does a princess live?

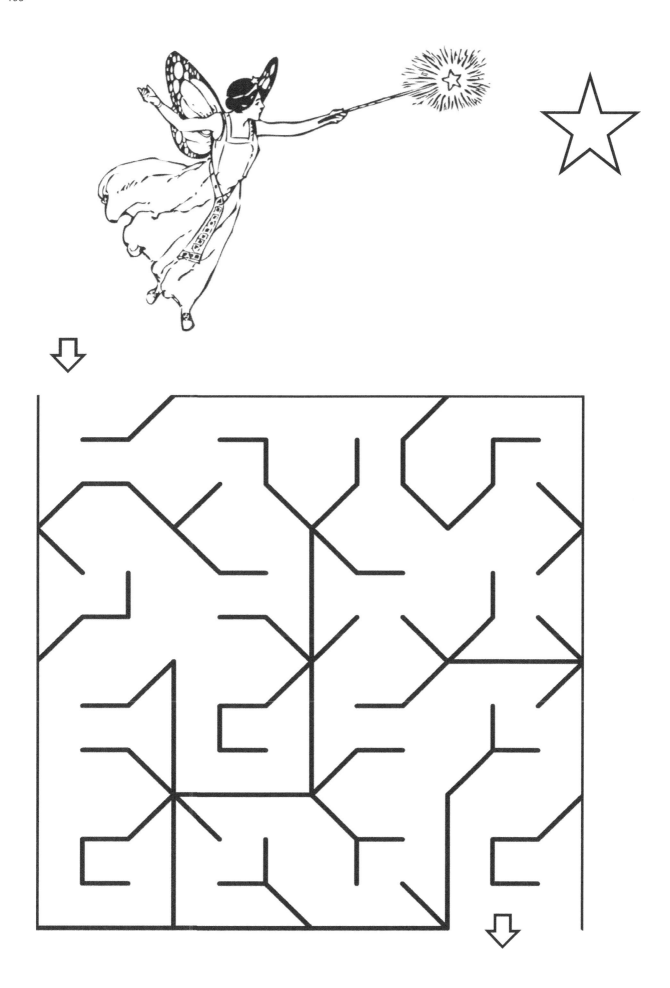

Who is Tinker Bell's friend?

Little Red Ridding Hood

Peter Pan

Mother Goose

Trace the letters by following the dots.

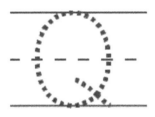

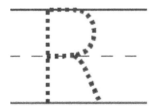

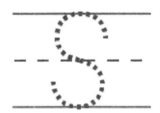

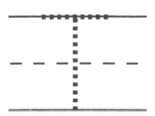

Draw a line to match the pictures.

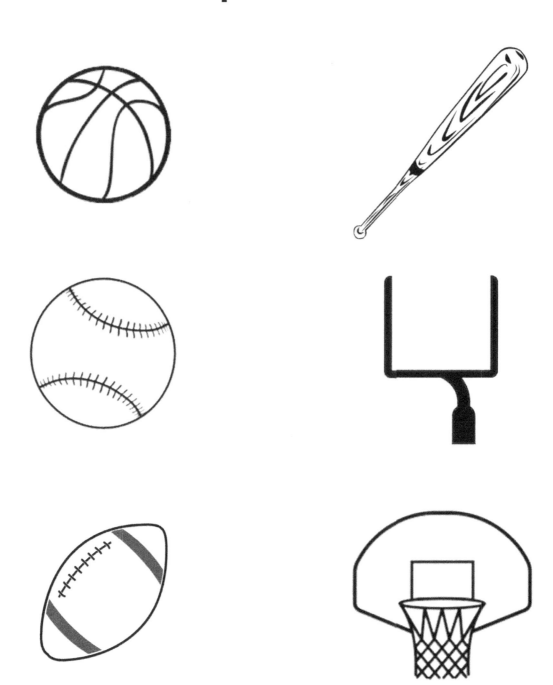

What kind of shoes do horses wear?

Trace the letters by following the dots.

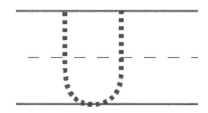

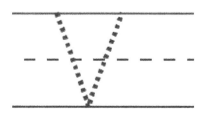

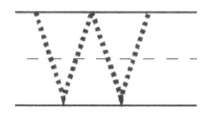

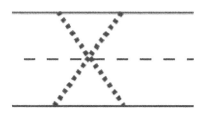

Do you eat your fruit and vegetables?

Yes

No

When should you wear a helmet?

When riding a bike.

When roller skating.

When riding a scooter.

Circle the friendly dogs.

Trace the letters by following the dots.

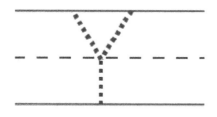

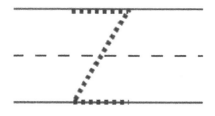

Which animal is called the unicorn of the sea?

Go over or under from start to finish.

Draw an elephant then color.

125

Which clown do you like?

Trace the numbers by following the dotted lines.

129

Draw a line to match the pictures.

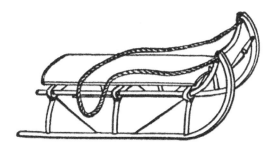

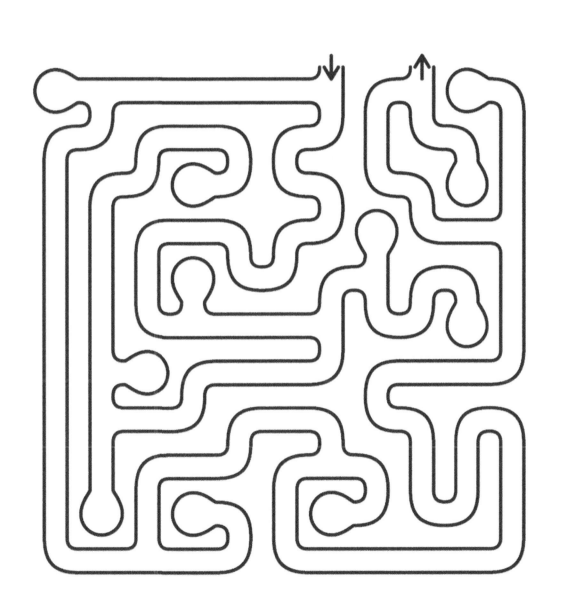

Which animals start with the letter S ?

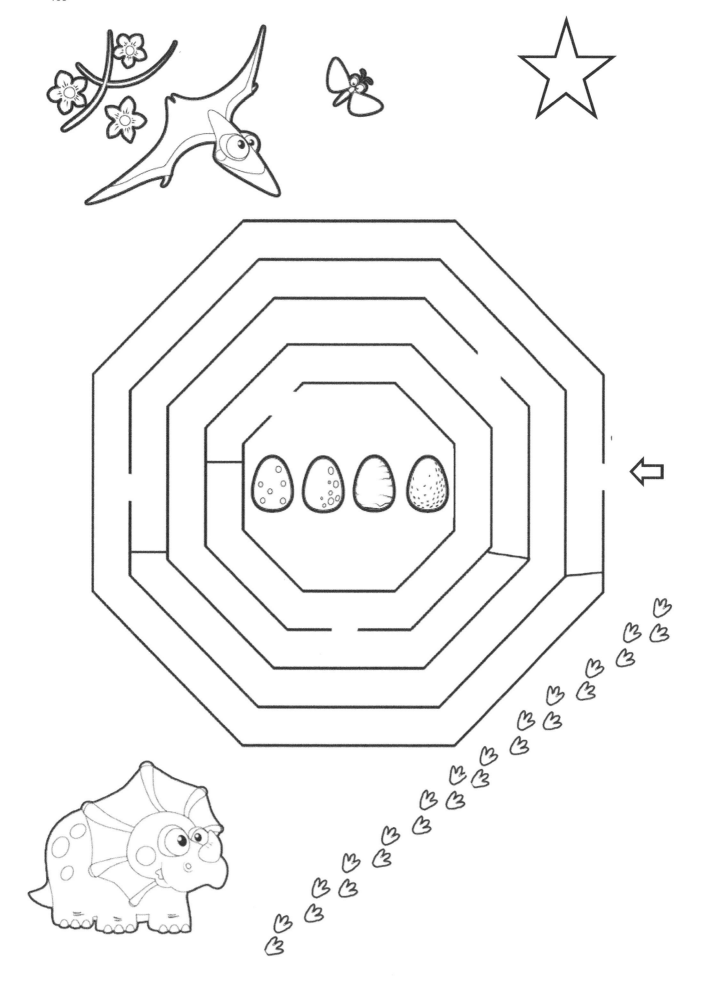

Circle the letter each picture starts with.

M R D

Which is your favorite nursey rhyme?

I'm a Little Teapot

Hickory Dickory Dock

There was an Old Woman Who Lived in a Shoe

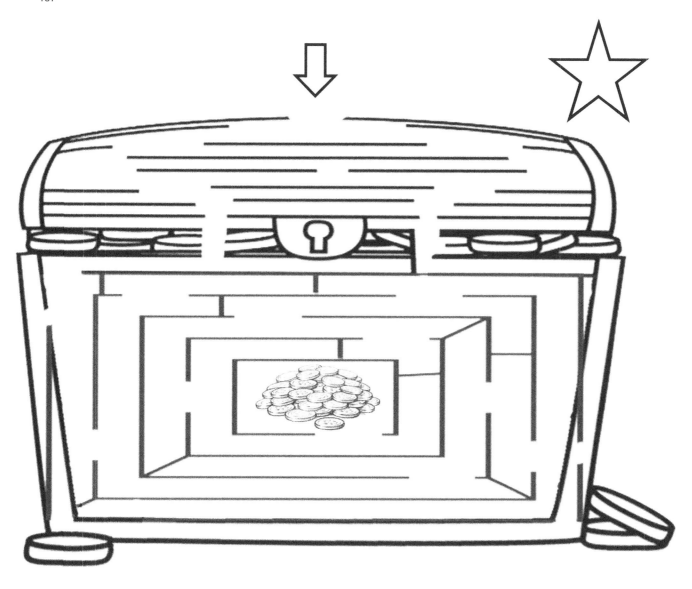

Trace the numbers by following the dotted lines.

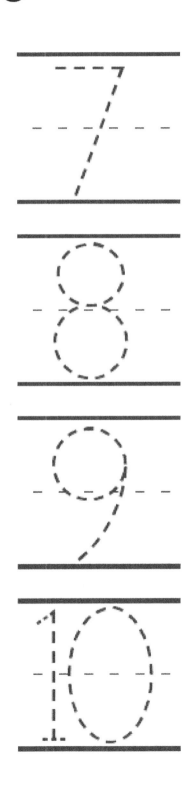

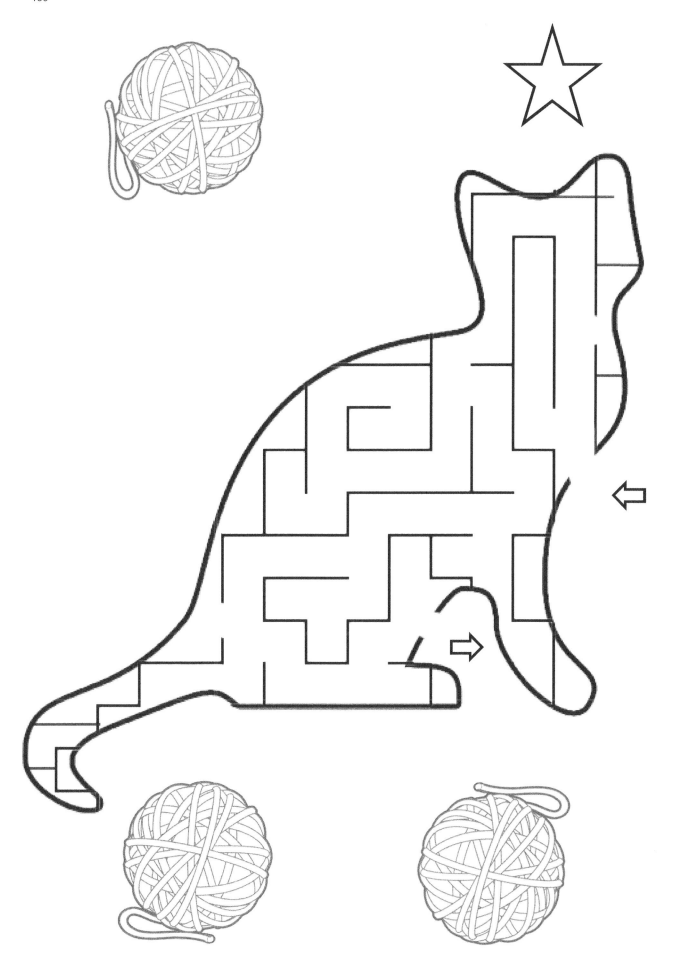

Spot the 5 differences.

Which picture does not belong?

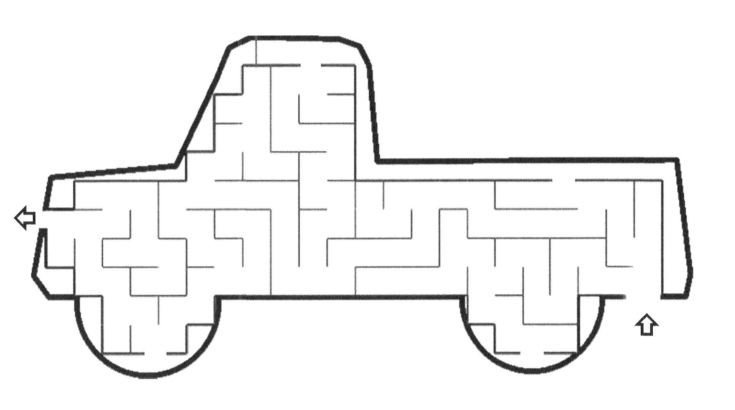

Fill in the blank with the missing letter.

_ar

_ruck

_lane

T C P

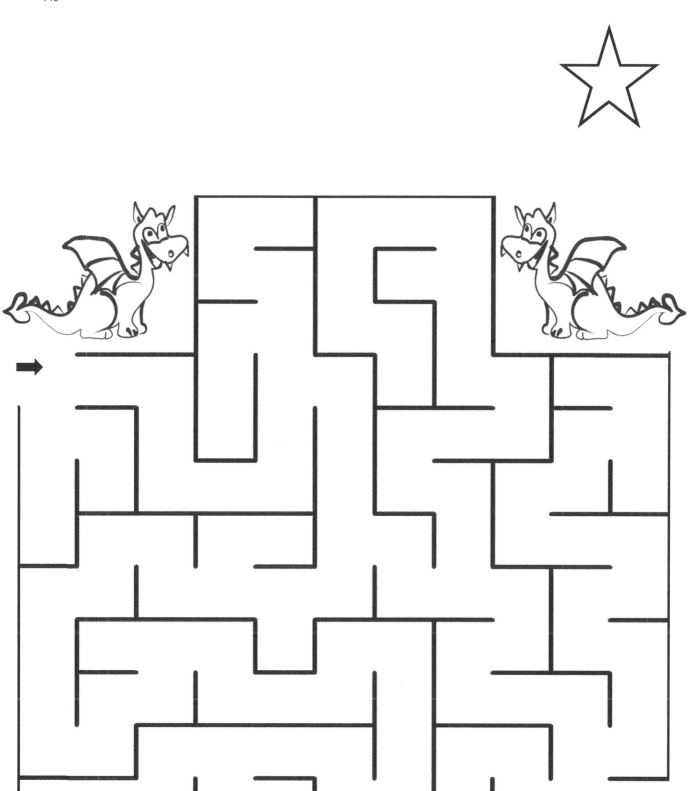

Draw a line to match the pictures.

Circle all the horses you can find.

Do you like to skate?

About the Author

John B. Tutor

As a teacher affectionately known as "Mr. Math", he's helped hundreds of students develop problem solving skills.

Armed with the motto "learning should be fun" and unwavering dedication he hopes to mold the minds of young learners everywhere with his Maze Master Activity Books for Kids.

Find his Toddler Mazes, Preschool Mazes and Kindergarten Maze books on Amazon.

Congratulations of a job well done!

_____

is awarded this certificate

Apprentice Maze Master

I completed this book on _____

and earned _____ gold stars.

Made in the USA
Monee, IL
22 May 2022